I want to color that!

I've heard that for many years from my friends who are privy to my works-in-progress. Whatever material I work with, it typically begins as a line drawing. Even when I am working on an oil painting - which I've been doing almost exclusively for the past few years, it begins with a line drawing on canvas. And I have to admit, even I get the urge to grab some crayons, markers, or colored pencils and sit on the floor and color it!

But this book isn't for me; it's for all of my friends who've encouraged me over the years, and have told me (on more than one occassion), "I want to color that!"

A big Thank You also goes to those who contributed to this book with their permission for me to feature them herein. If you're around town, check out some of the people and businesses that are presented within these pages - you won't be disappointed!

I hope you have as much fun coloring this as I have had drawing it!

R. Antolic

Rick Antolic gives his sincere thanks to Kennywood for its invaluable assistance and cooperation in creating this book.

Pittsburgh

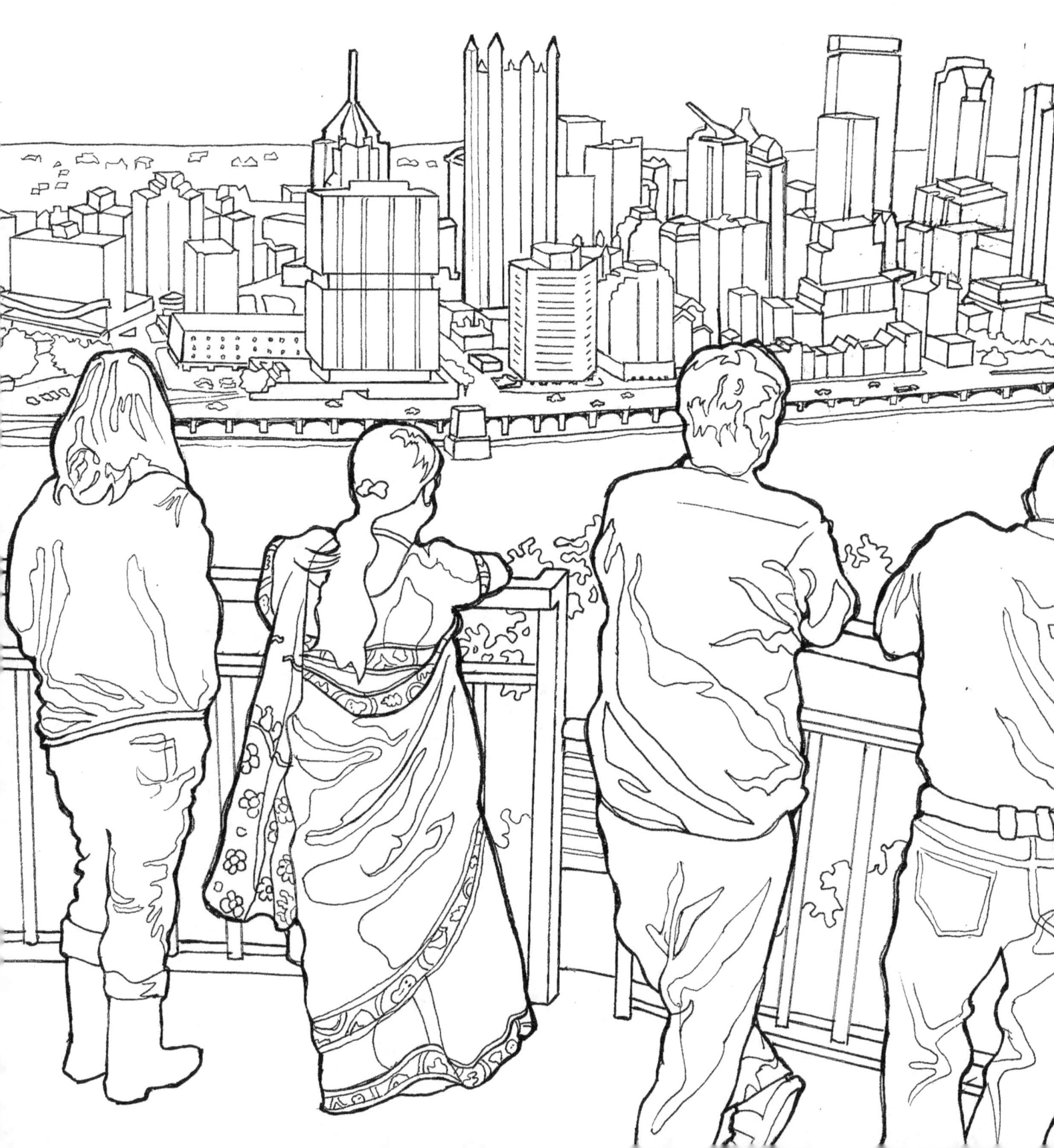

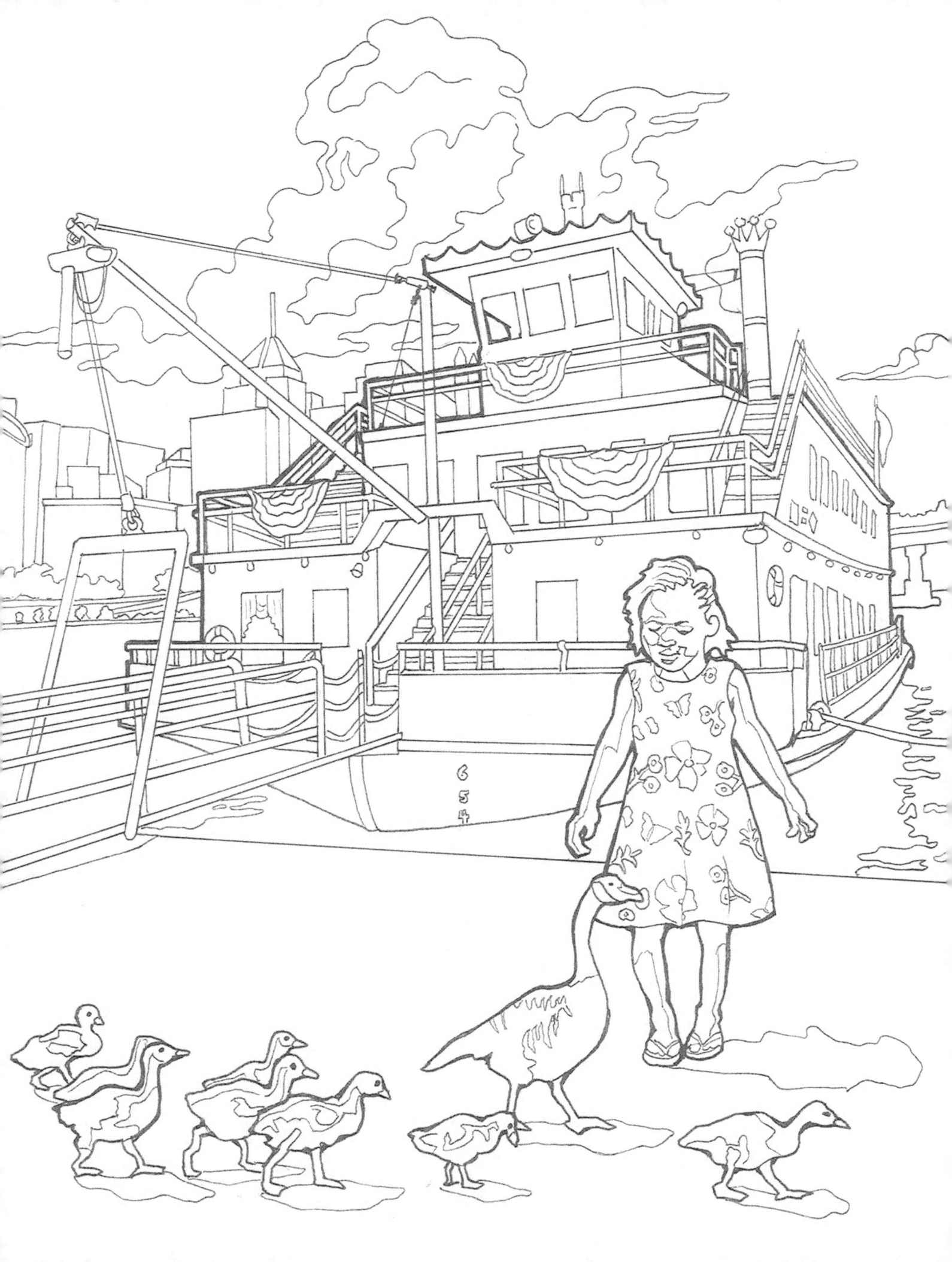

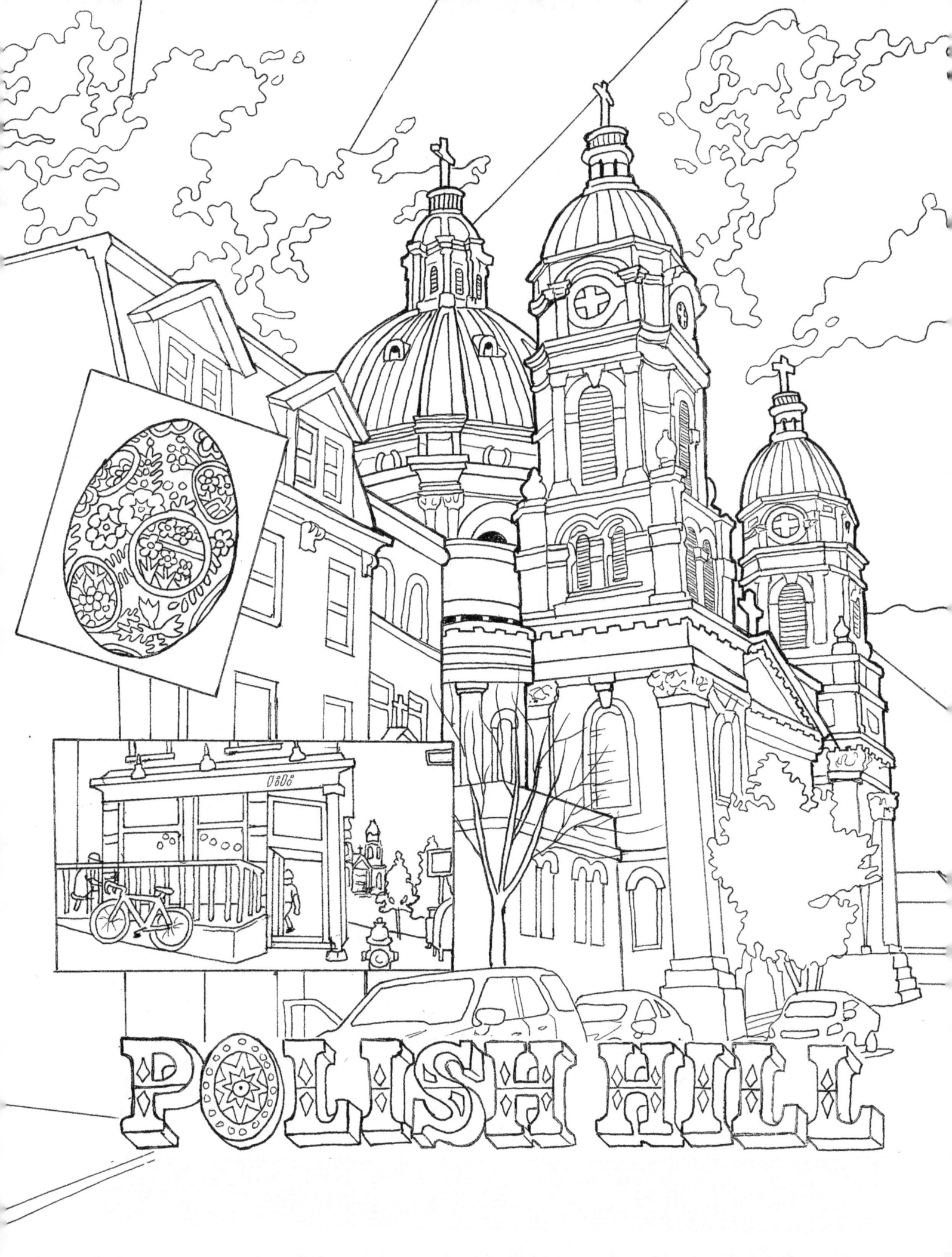

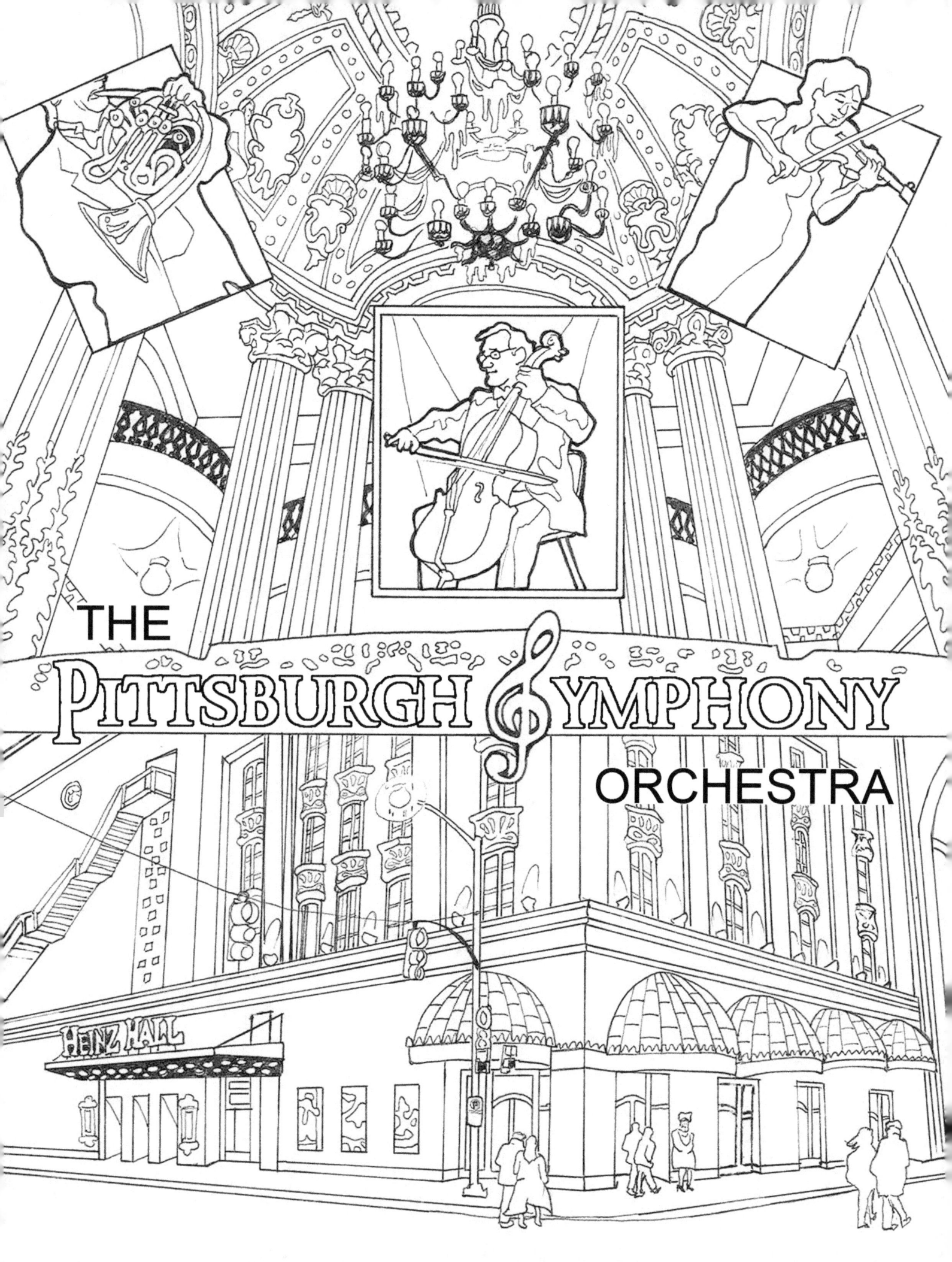

THE **PITTSBURGH** 𝄞 **YMPHONY**

ORCHESTRA

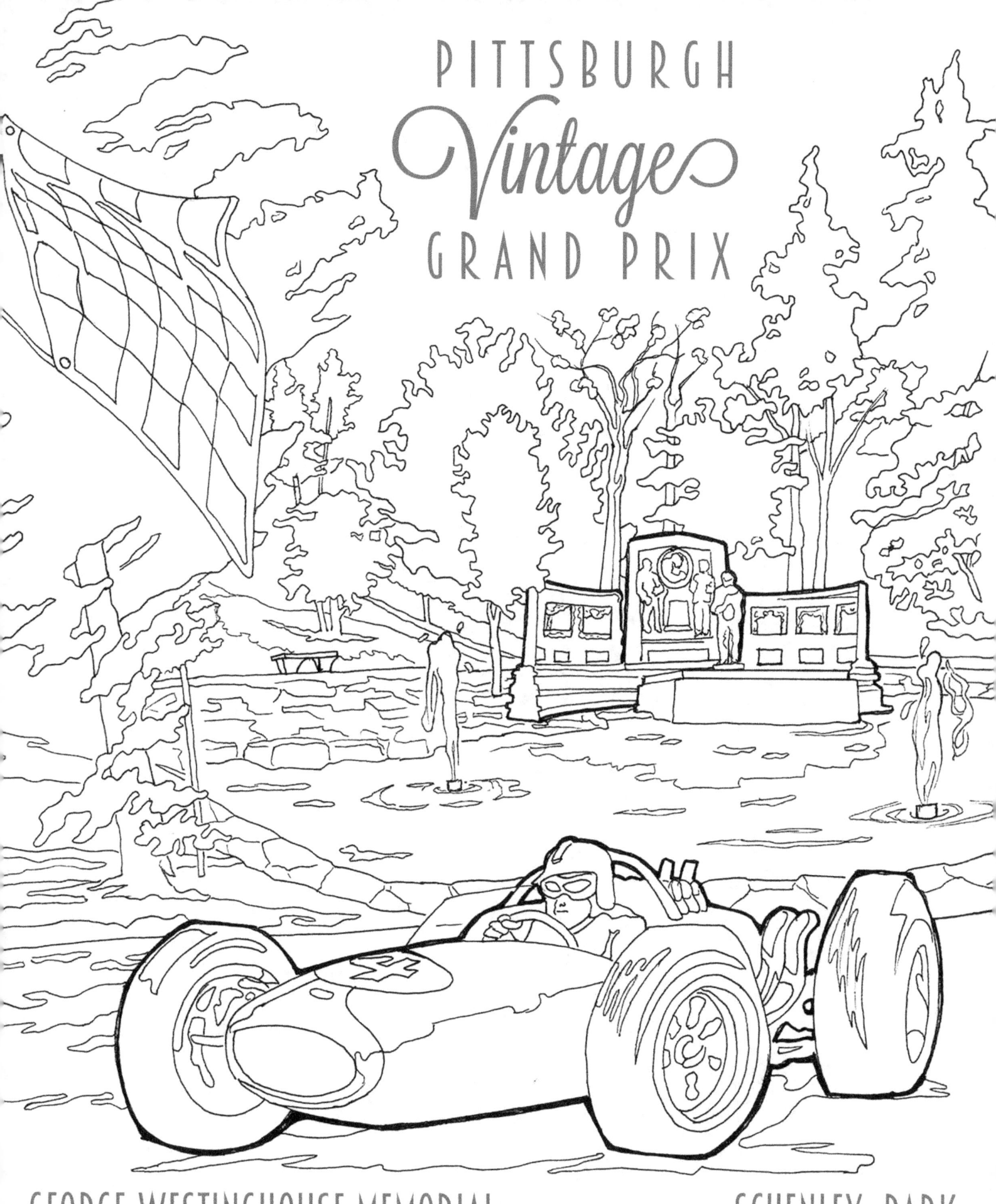

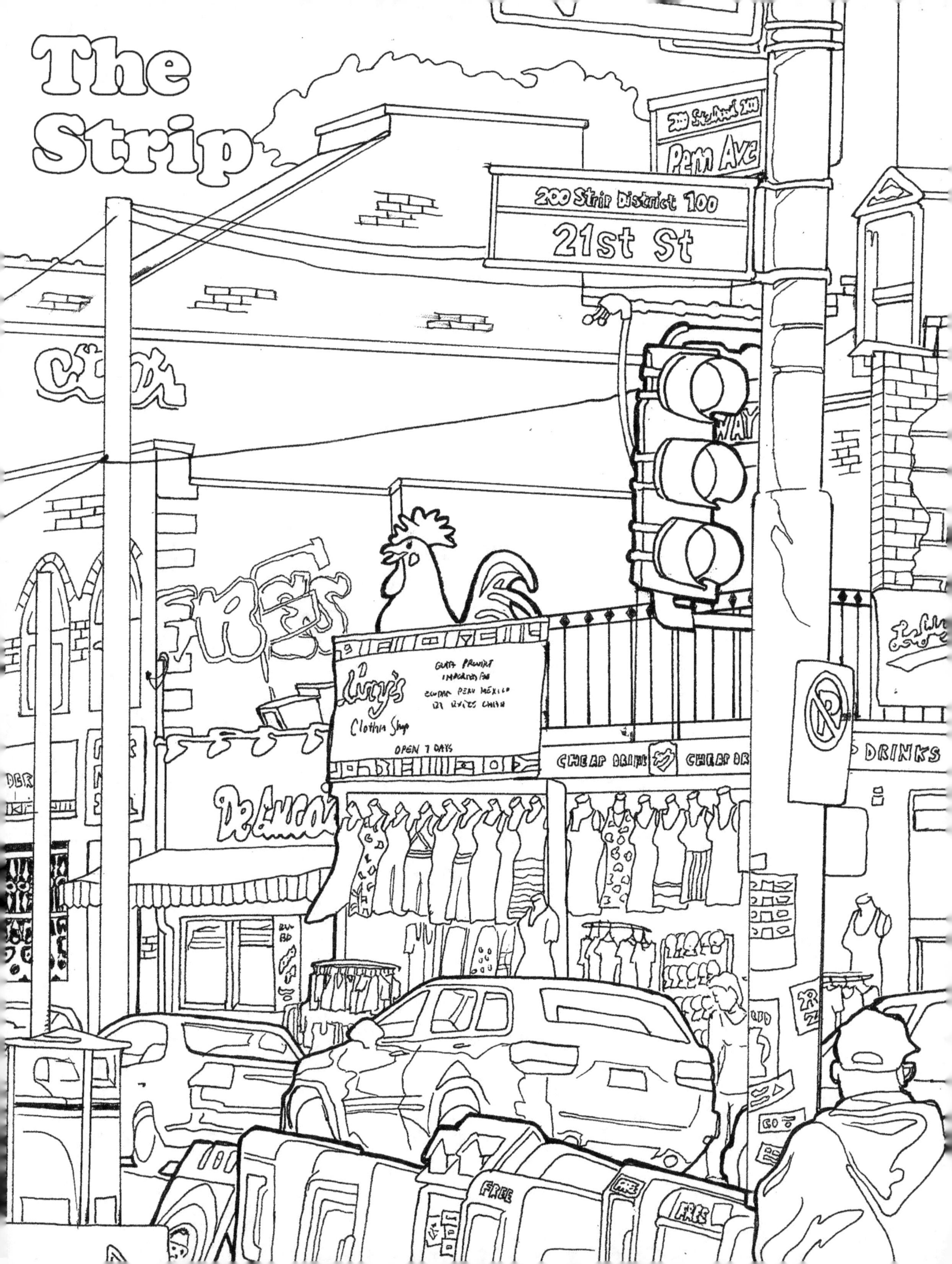

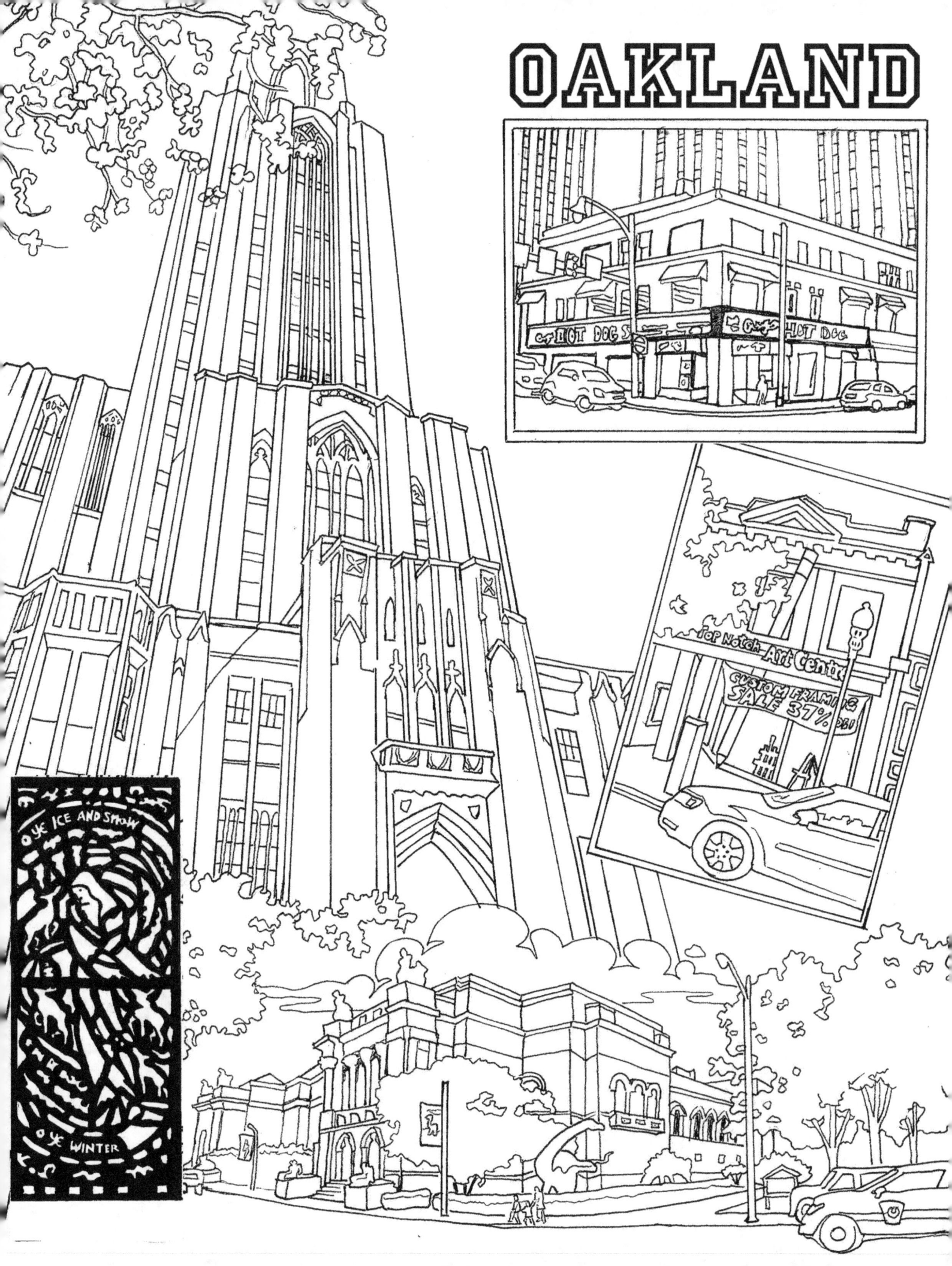

OAKLAND

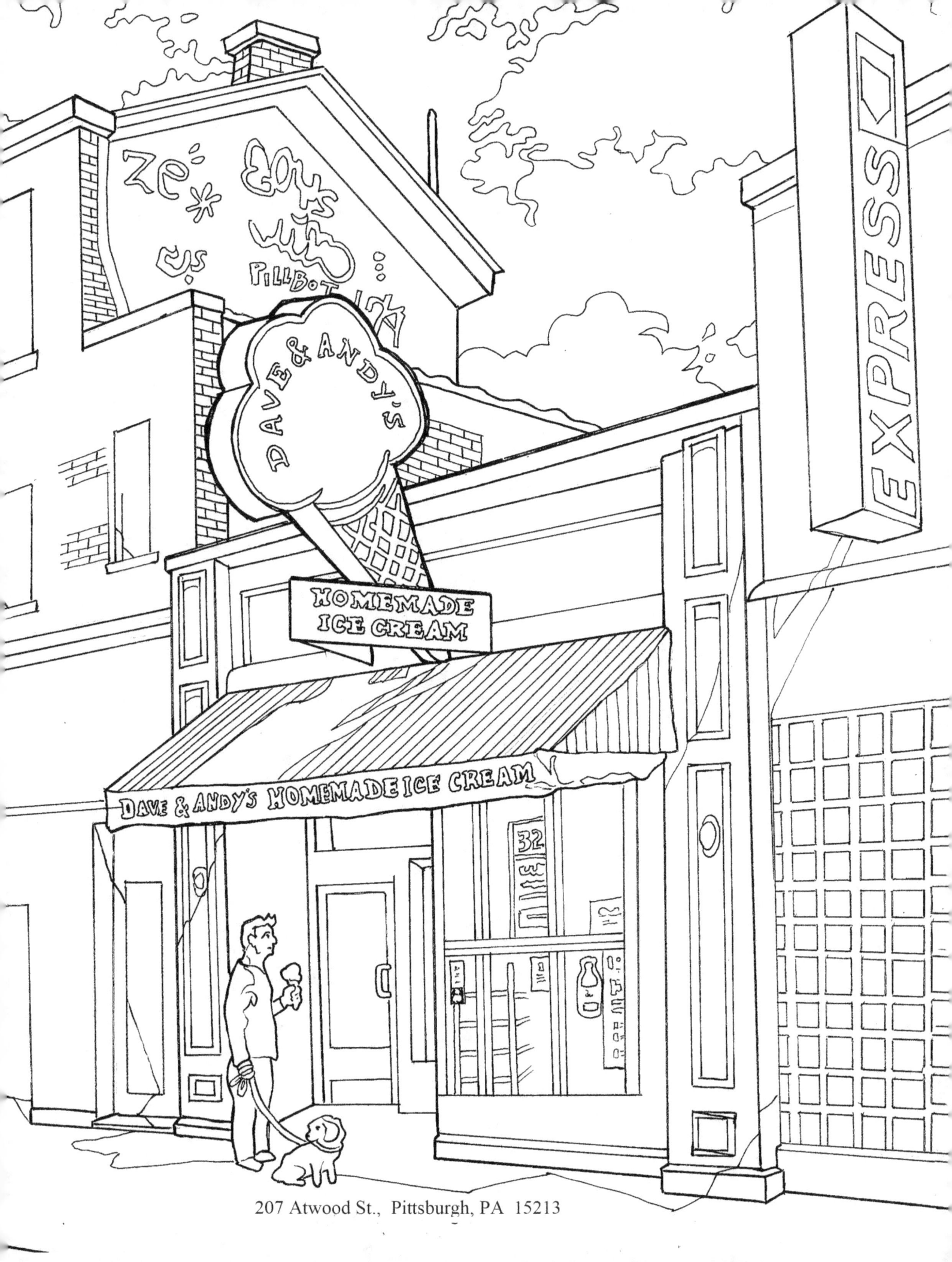

207 Atwood St., Pittsburgh, PA 15213

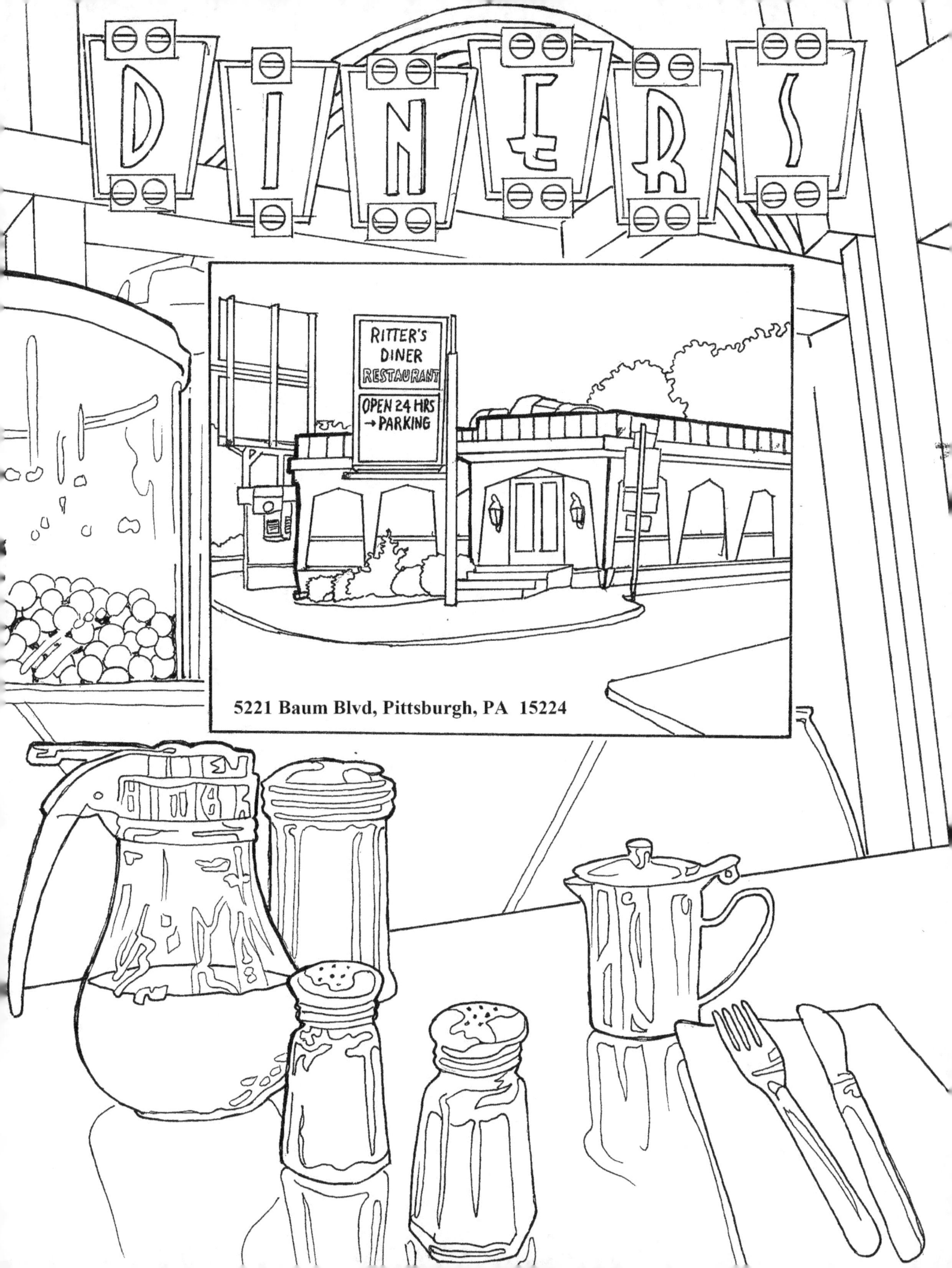

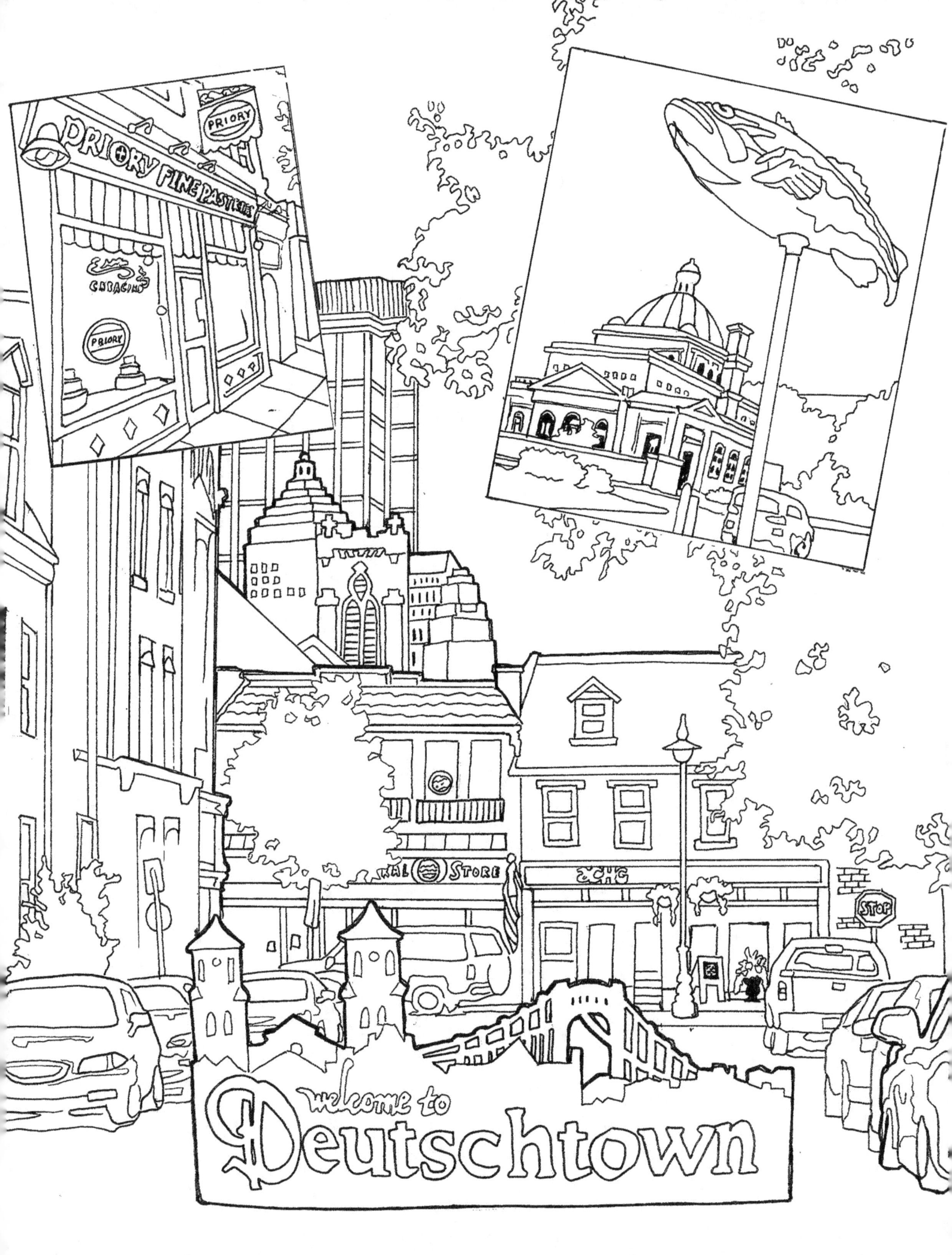

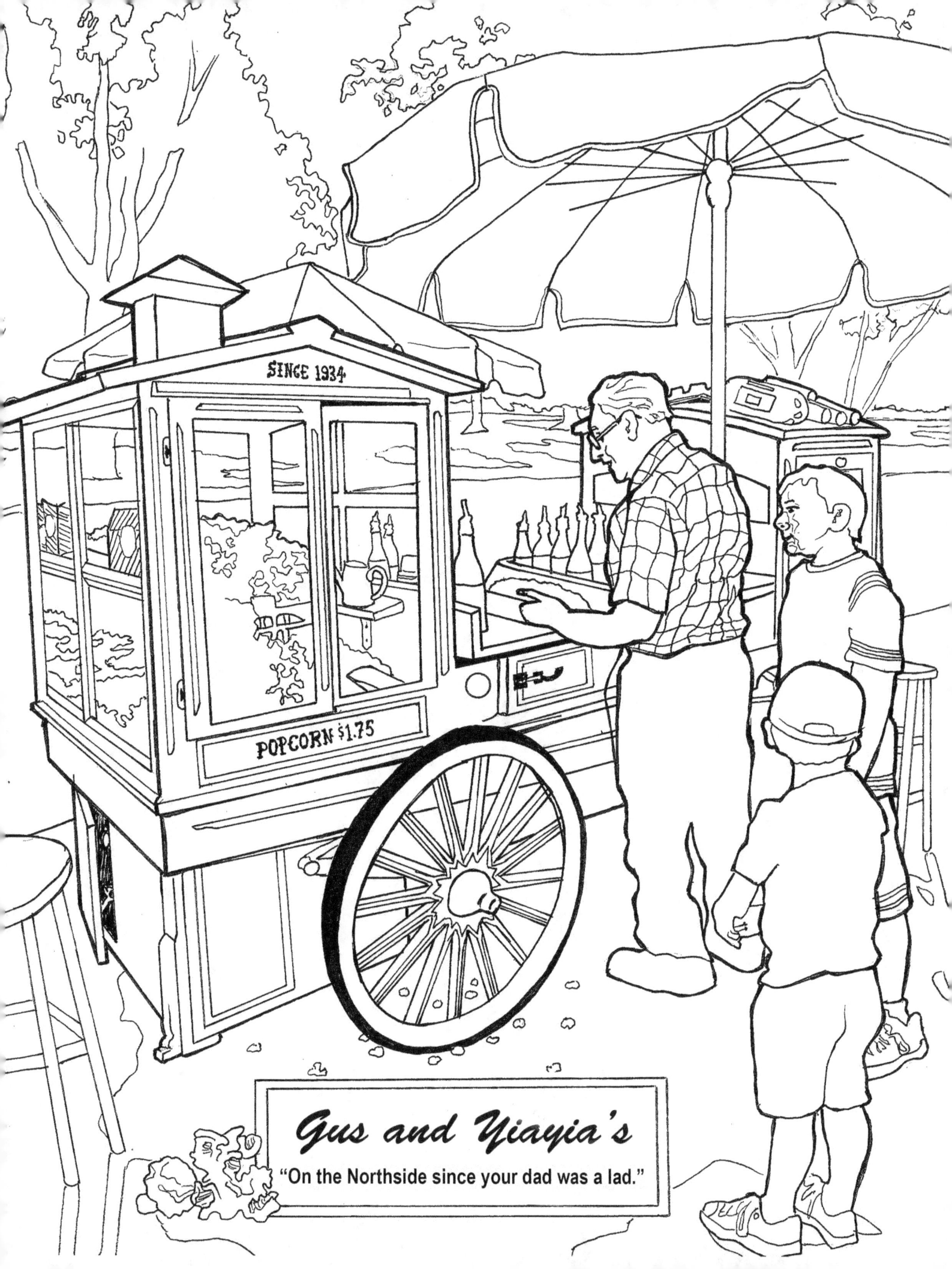

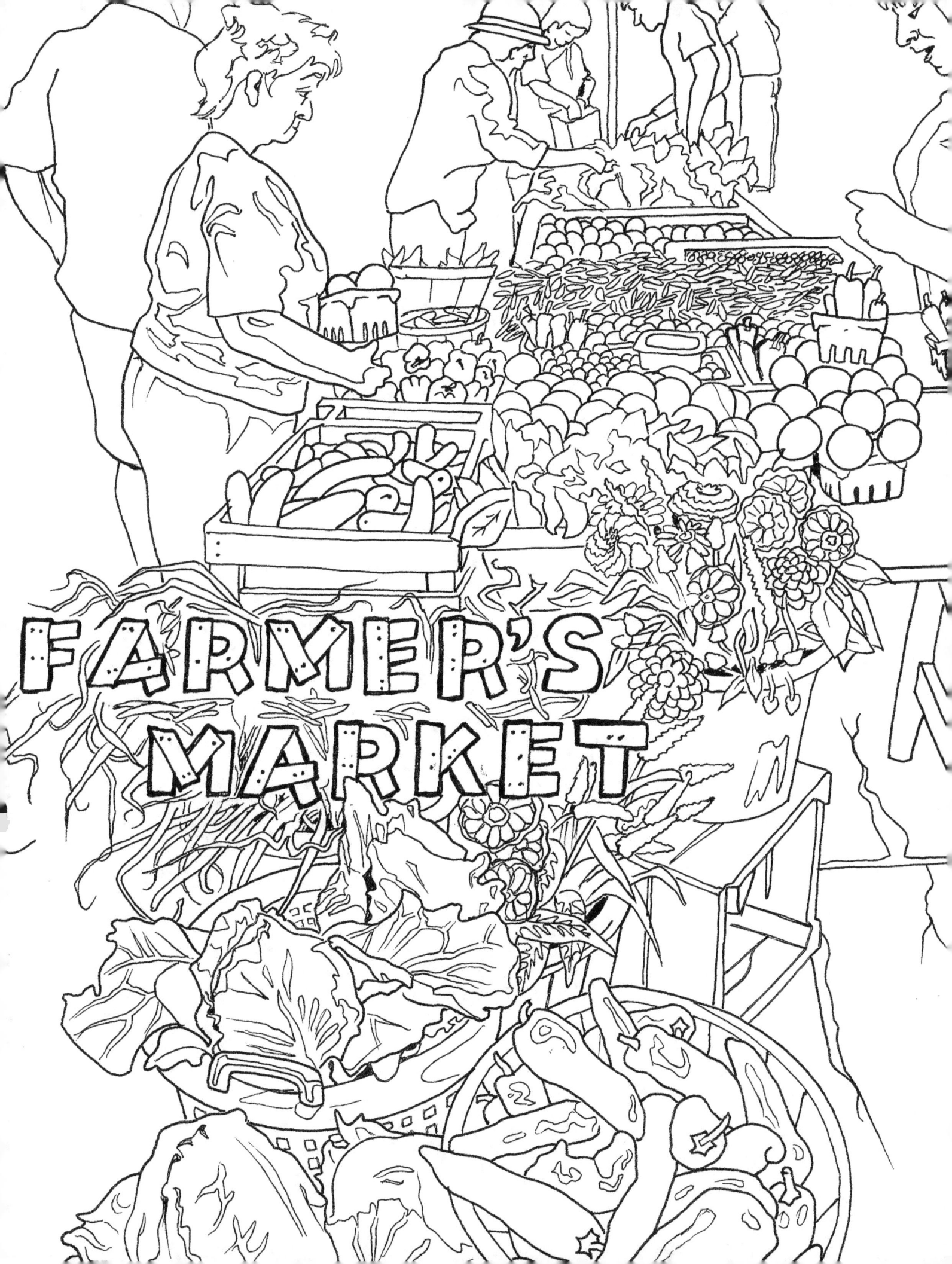

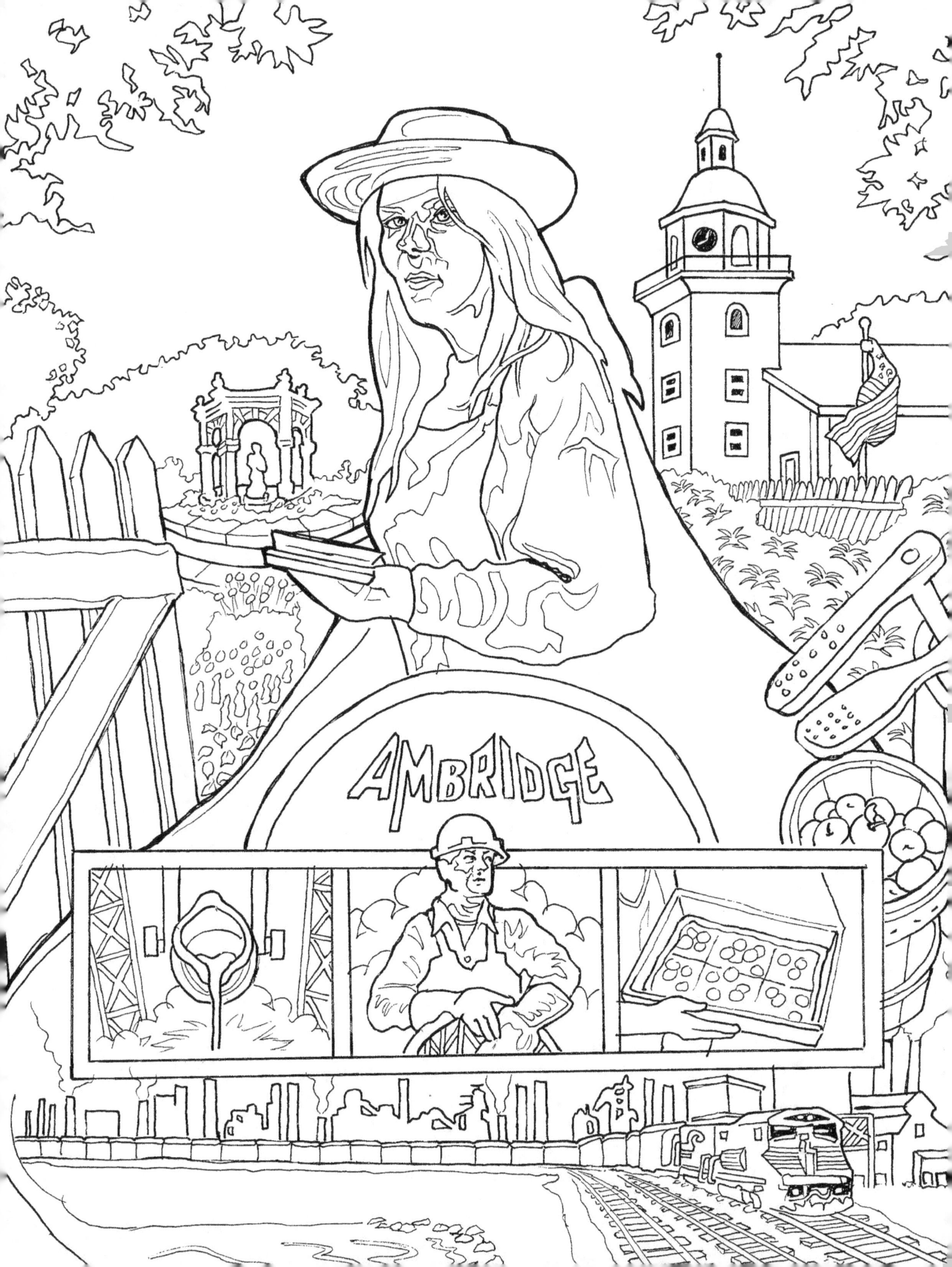

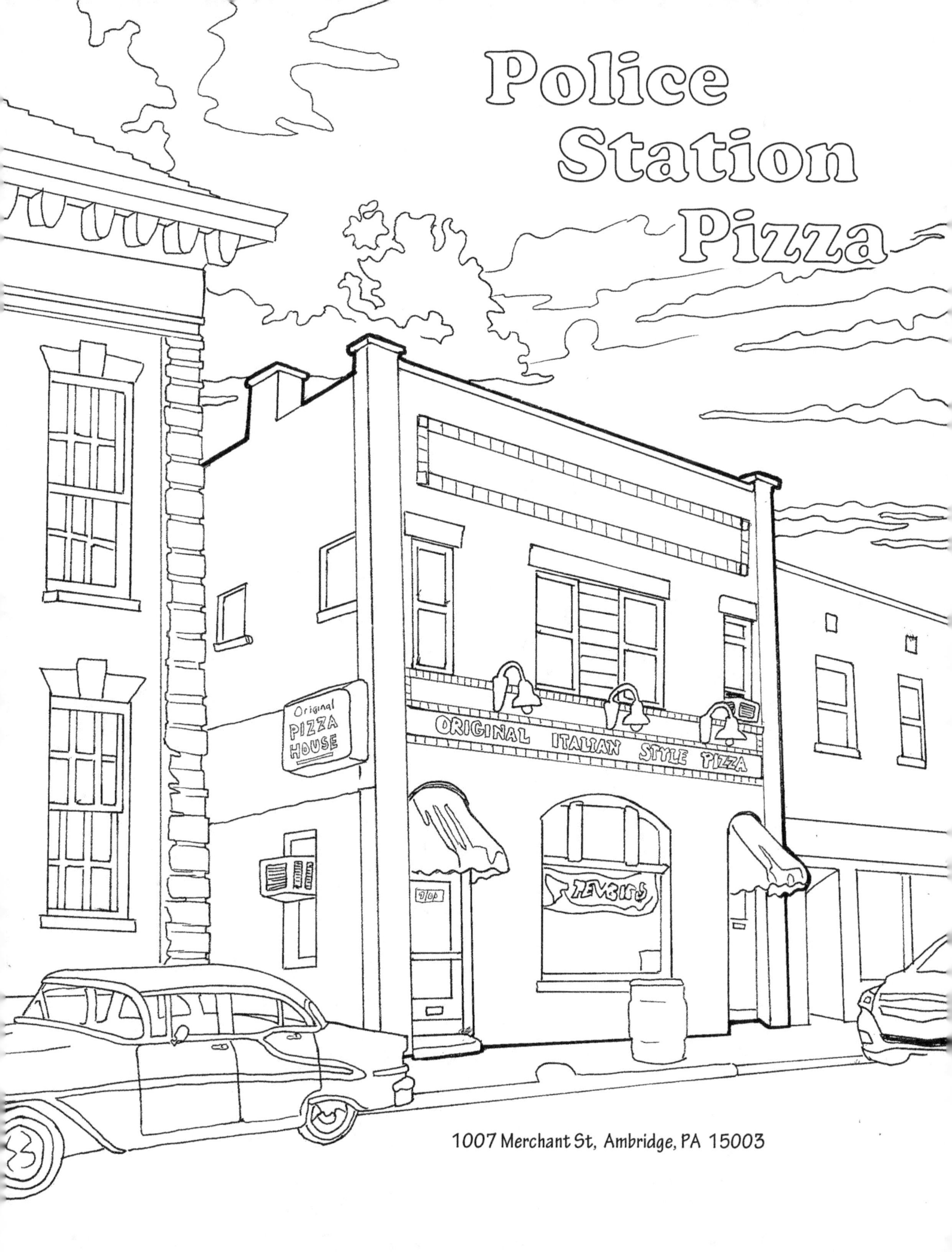

Police Station Pizza

1007 Merchant St, Ambridge, PA 15003

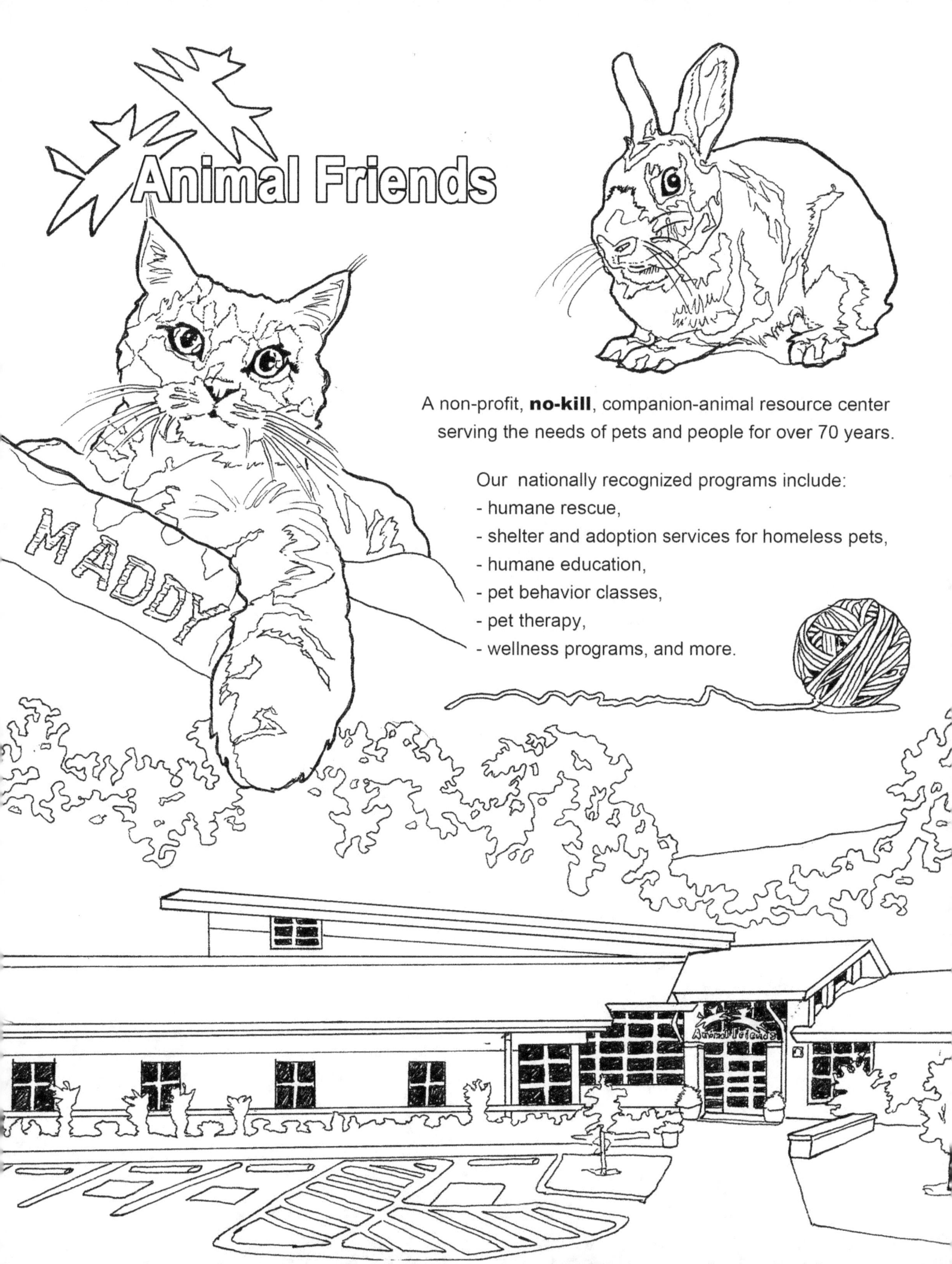

Animal Friends

A non-profit, **no-kill**, companion-animal resource center serving the needs of pets and people for over 70 years.

Our nationally recognized programs include:
- humane rescue,
- shelter and adoption services for homeless pets,
- humane education,
- pet behavior classes,
- pet therapy,
- wellness programs, and more.

MADDY

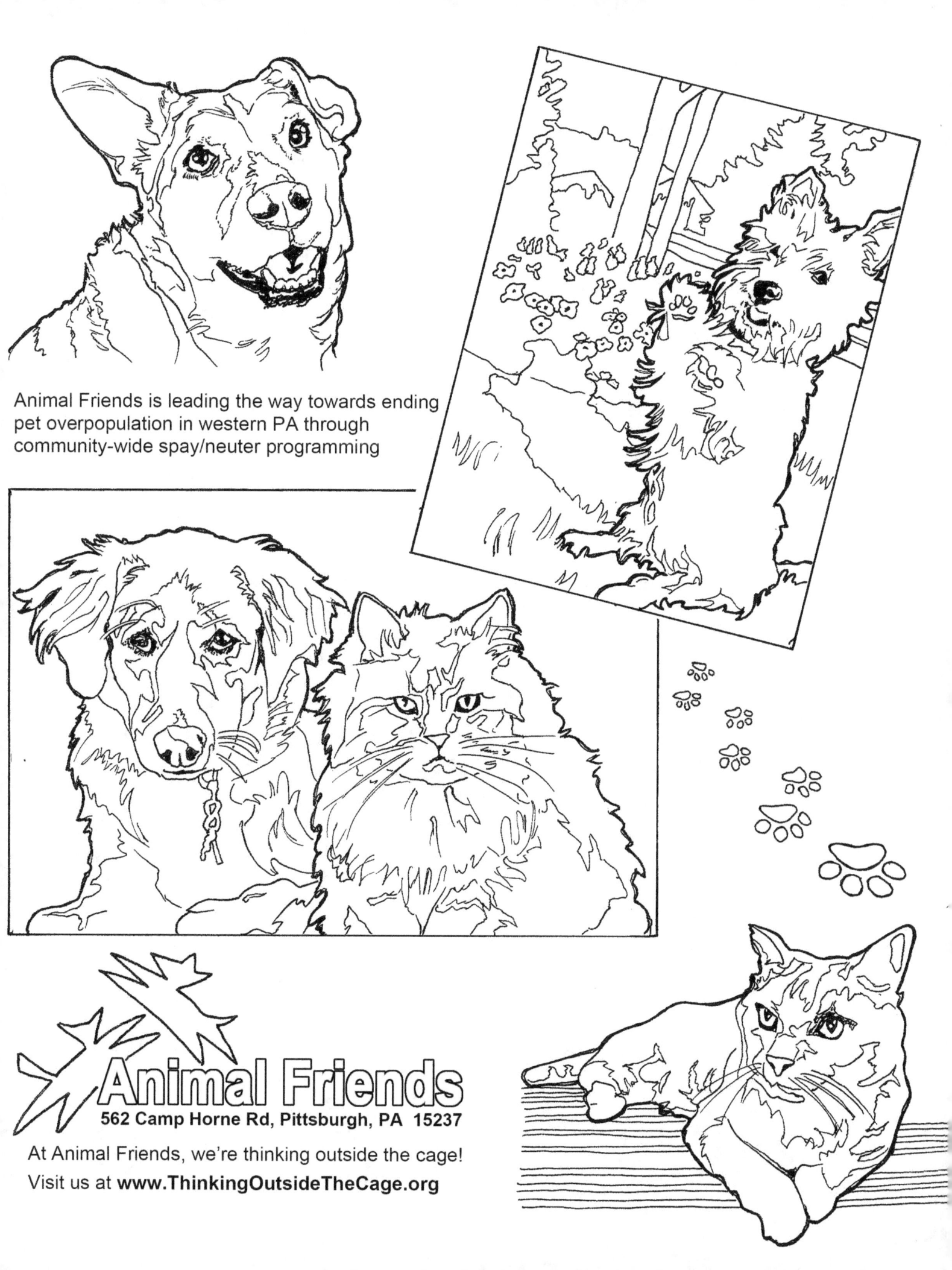

Animal Friends is leading the way towards ending pet overpopulation in western PA through community-wide spay/neuter programming

Animal Friends
562 Camp Horne Rd, Pittsburgh, PA 15237

At Animal Friends, we're thinking outside the cage!
Visit us at **www.ThinkingOutsideTheCage.org**

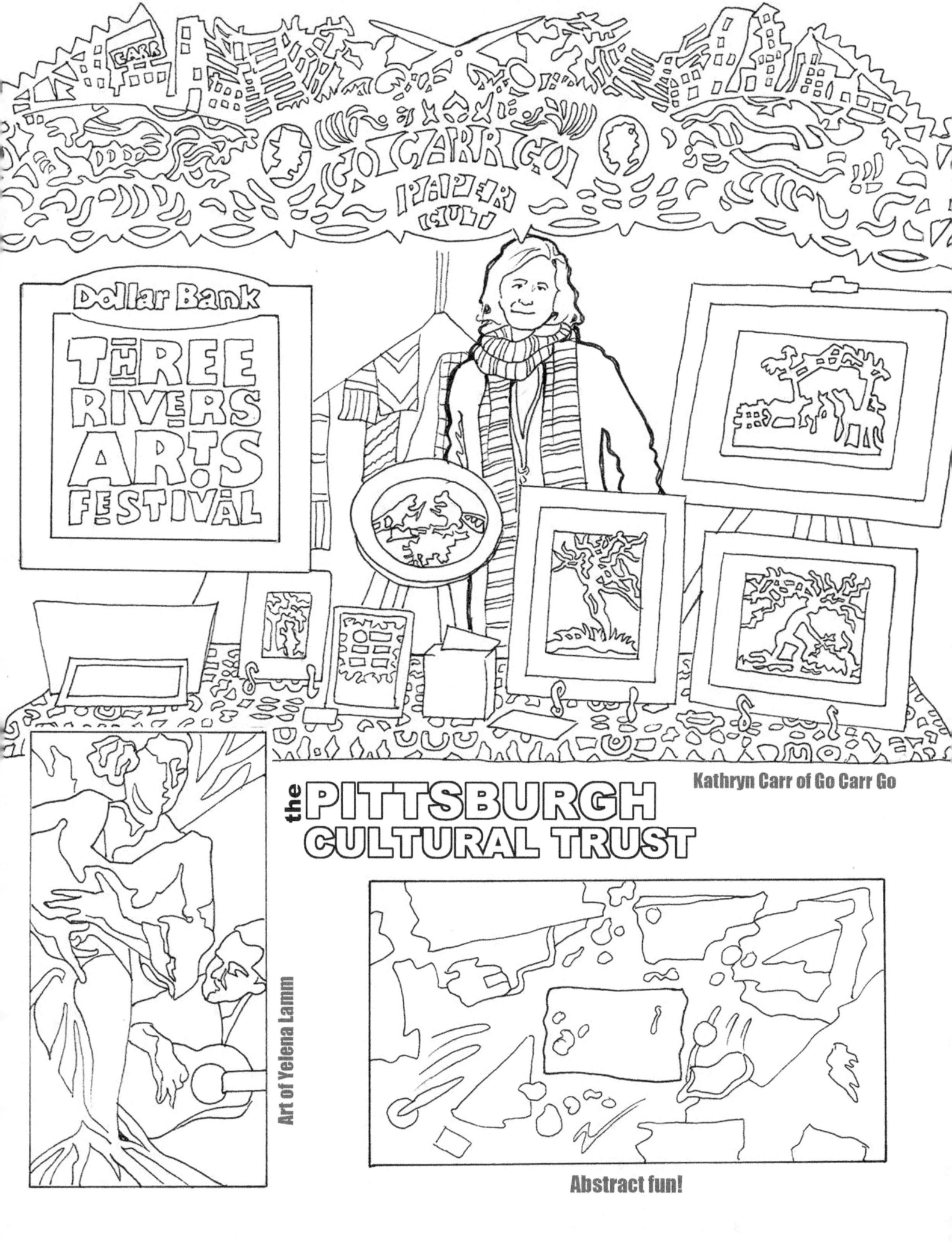

Dollar Bank

THREE RIVERS ARTS FESTIVAL

GO CARR GO
PAPER CUT

Kathryn Carr of Go Carr Go

the PITTSBURGH CULTURAL TRUST

Art of Yelena Lamm

Abstract fun!

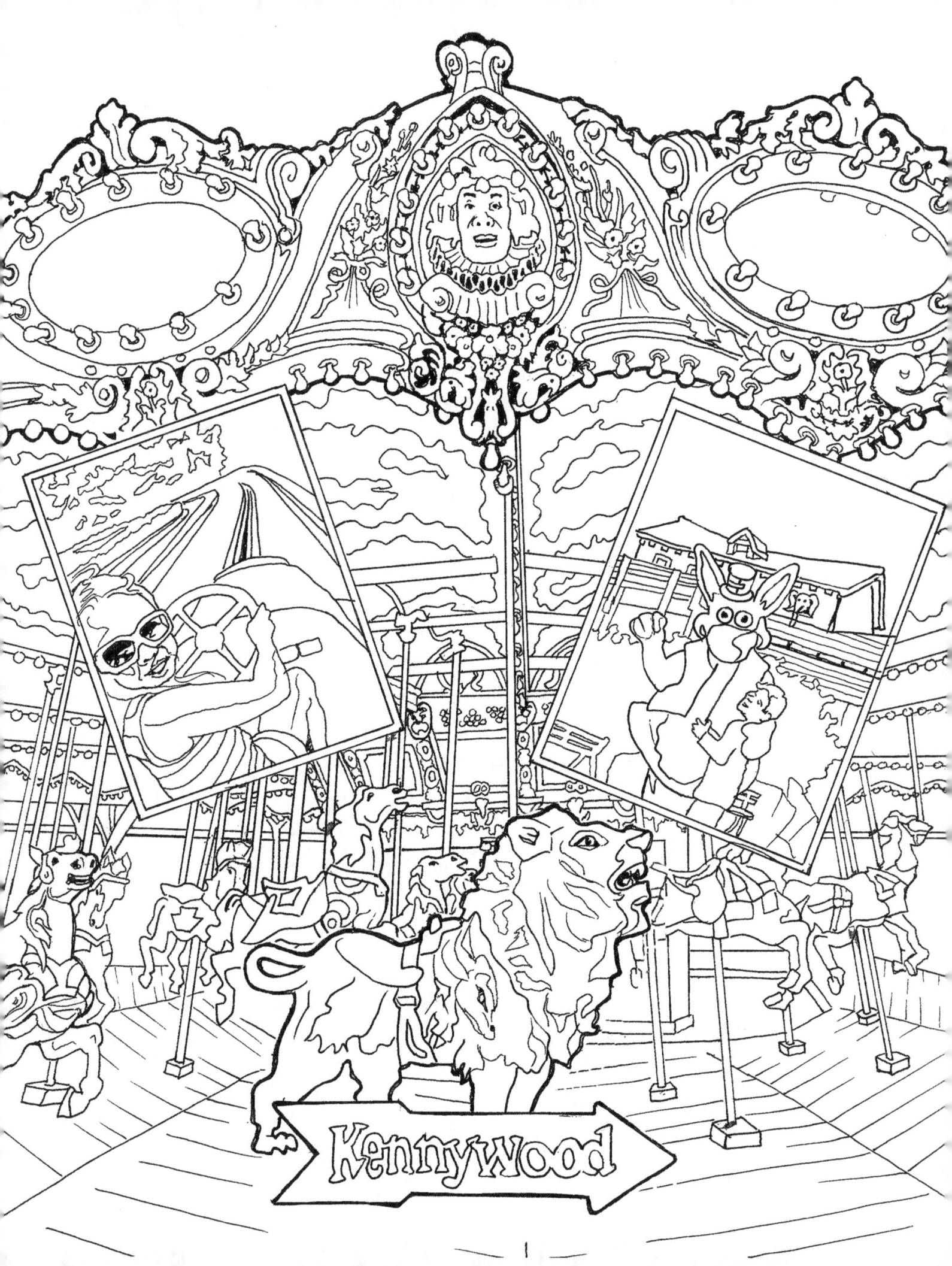

James Street Tavern

422 FORELAND ST.
PGH, PA 15212

BACK WITH A NEW SHOW
PAUL COSENTINO &

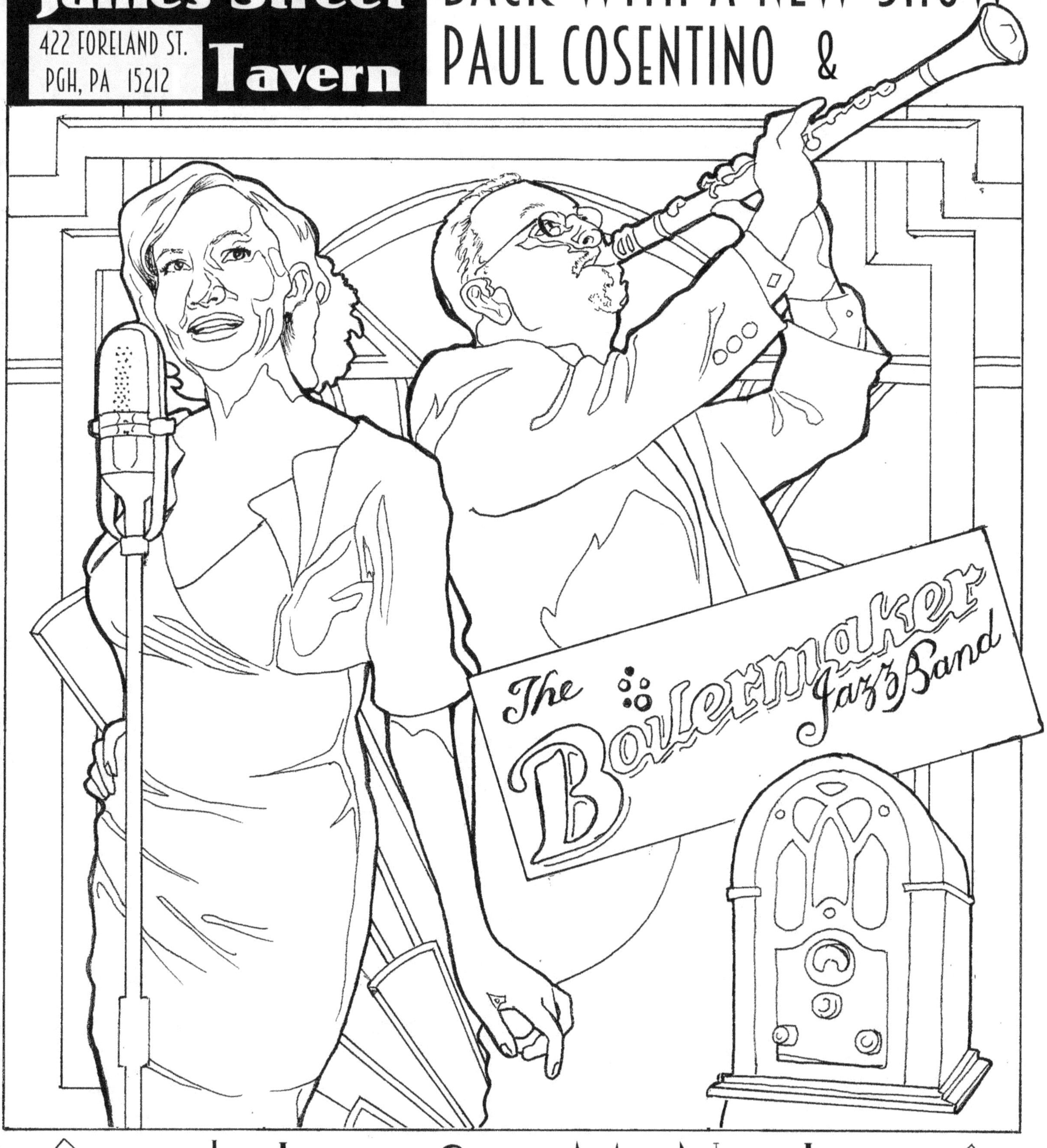

The Boilermaker Jazz Band

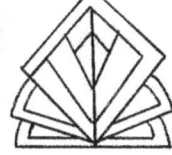 with Jennifer McNaulty

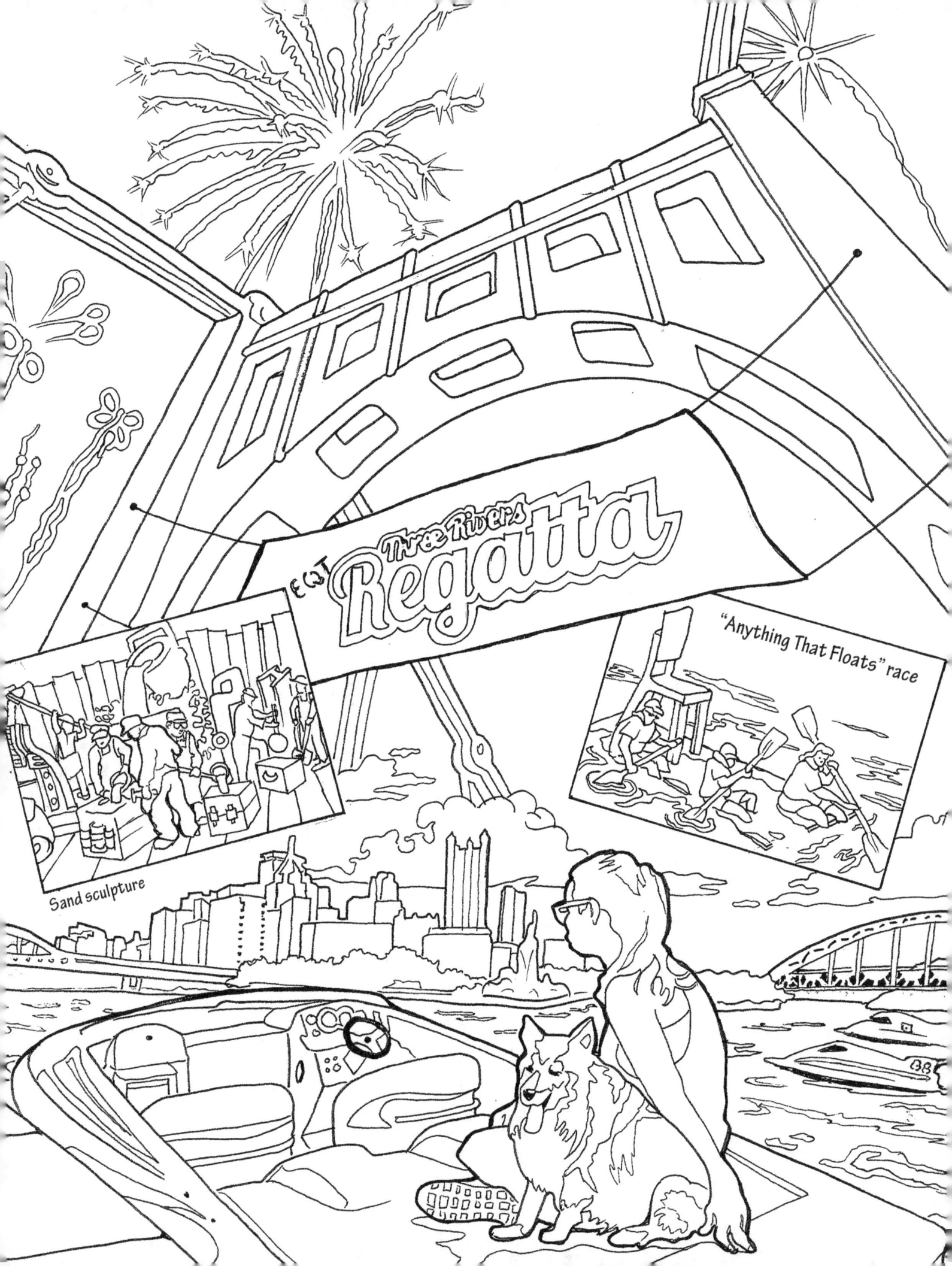

EQT Three Rivers Regatta

Sand sculpture

"Anything That Floats" race

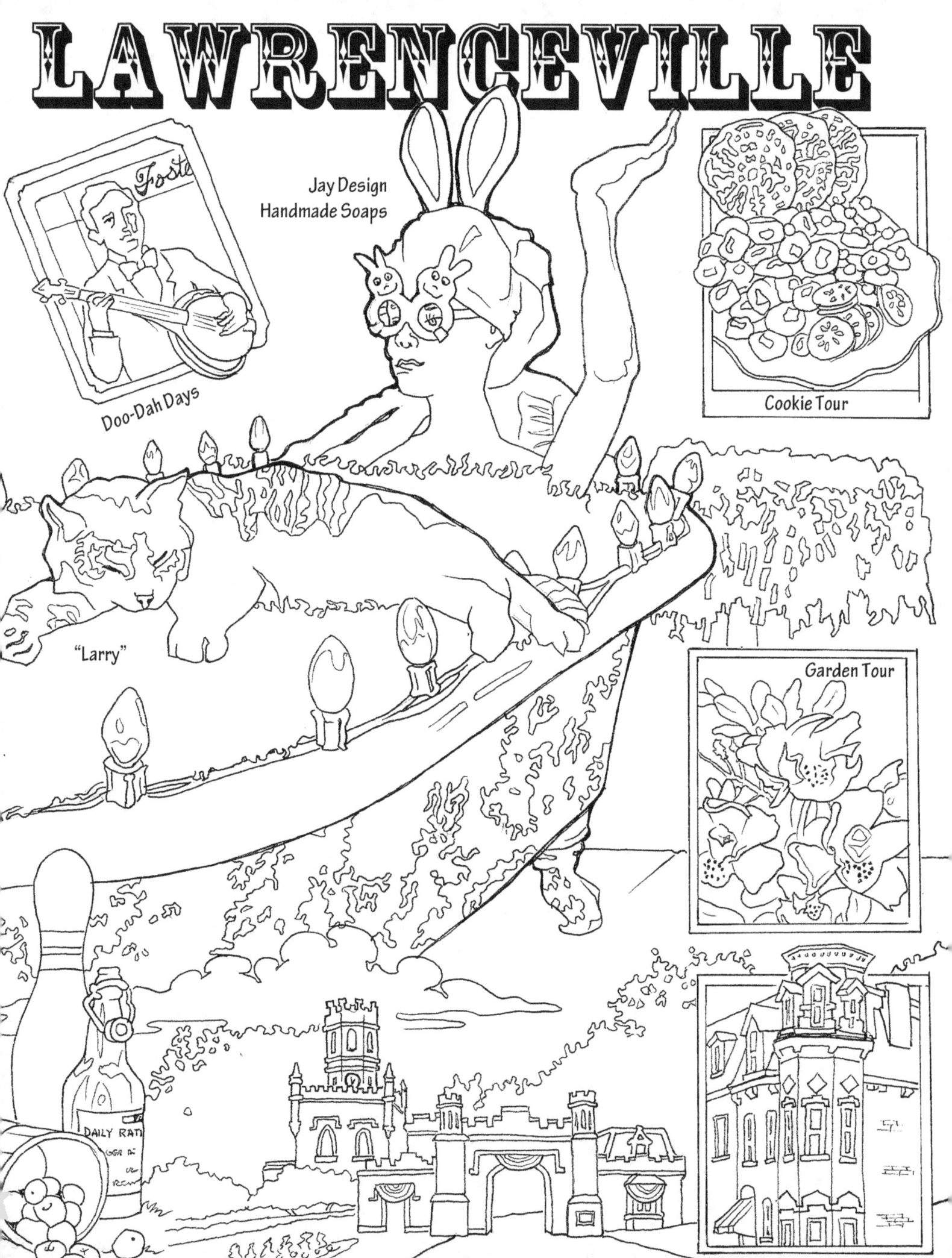

LAWRENCEVILLE

Jay Design
Handmade Soaps

Foste

Doo-Dah Days

Cookie Tour

"Larry"

Garden Tour

DAILY RAT

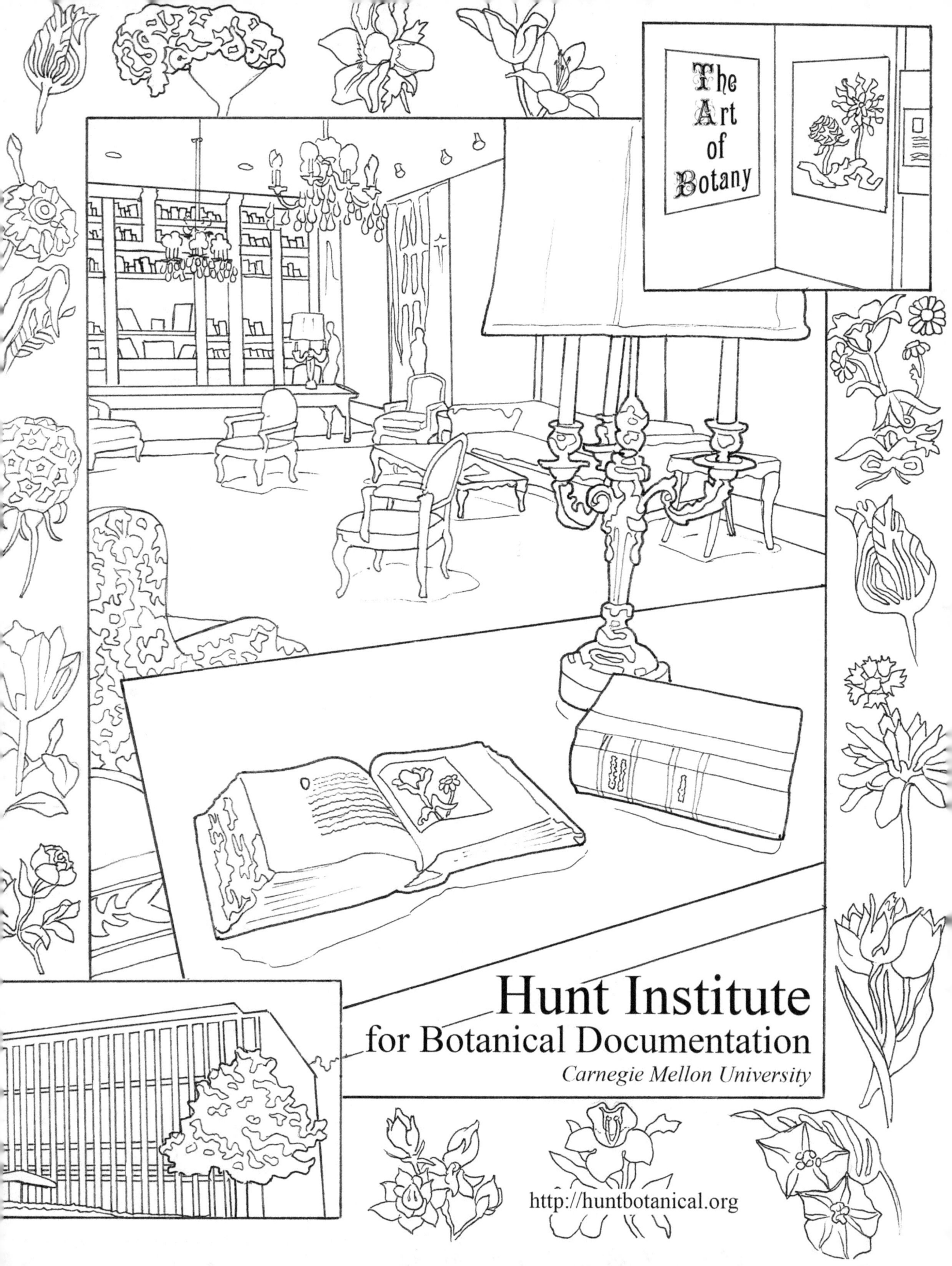

The Art of Botany

Hunt Institute

for Botanical Documentation

Carnegie Mellon University

http://huntbotanical.org

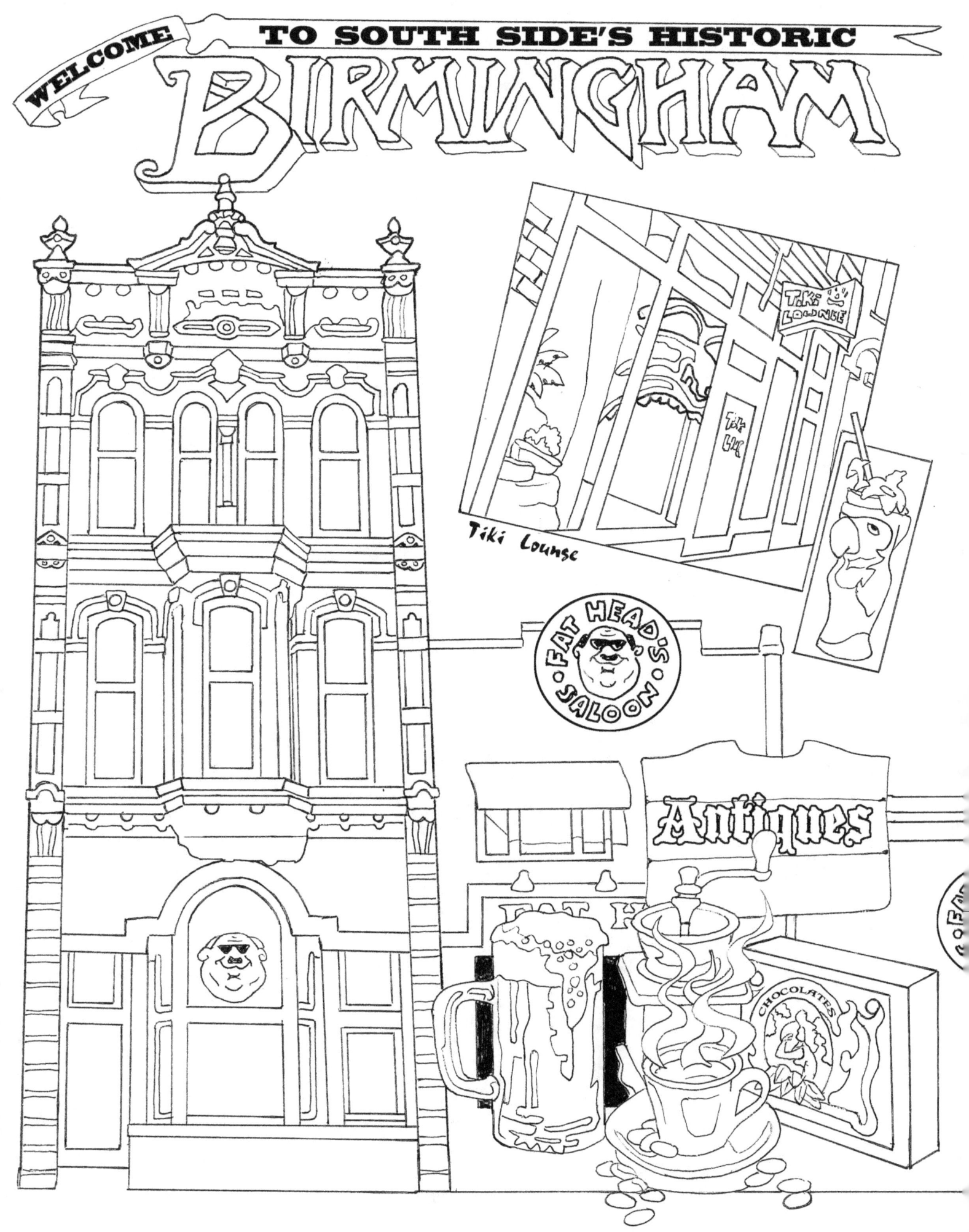

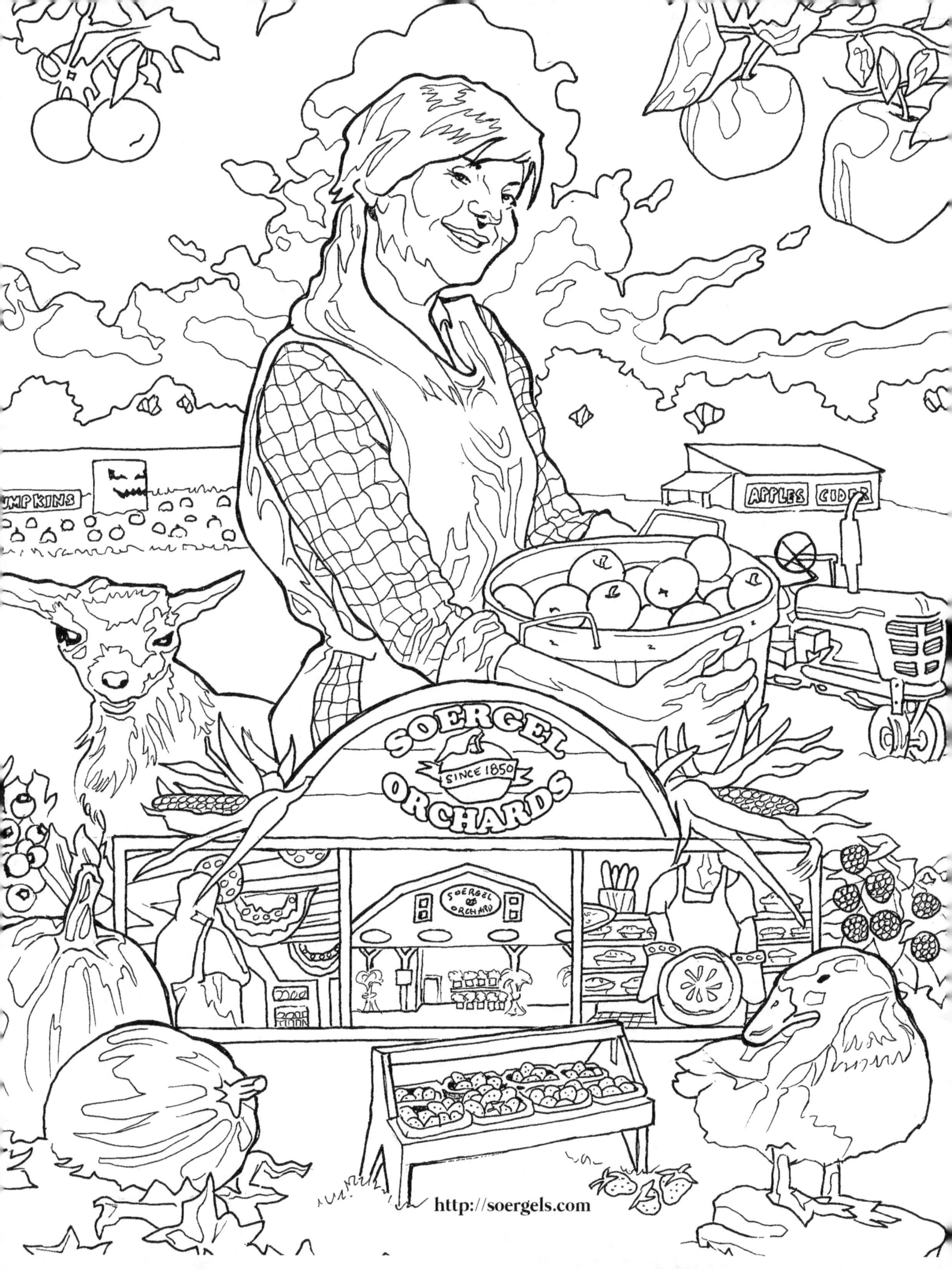

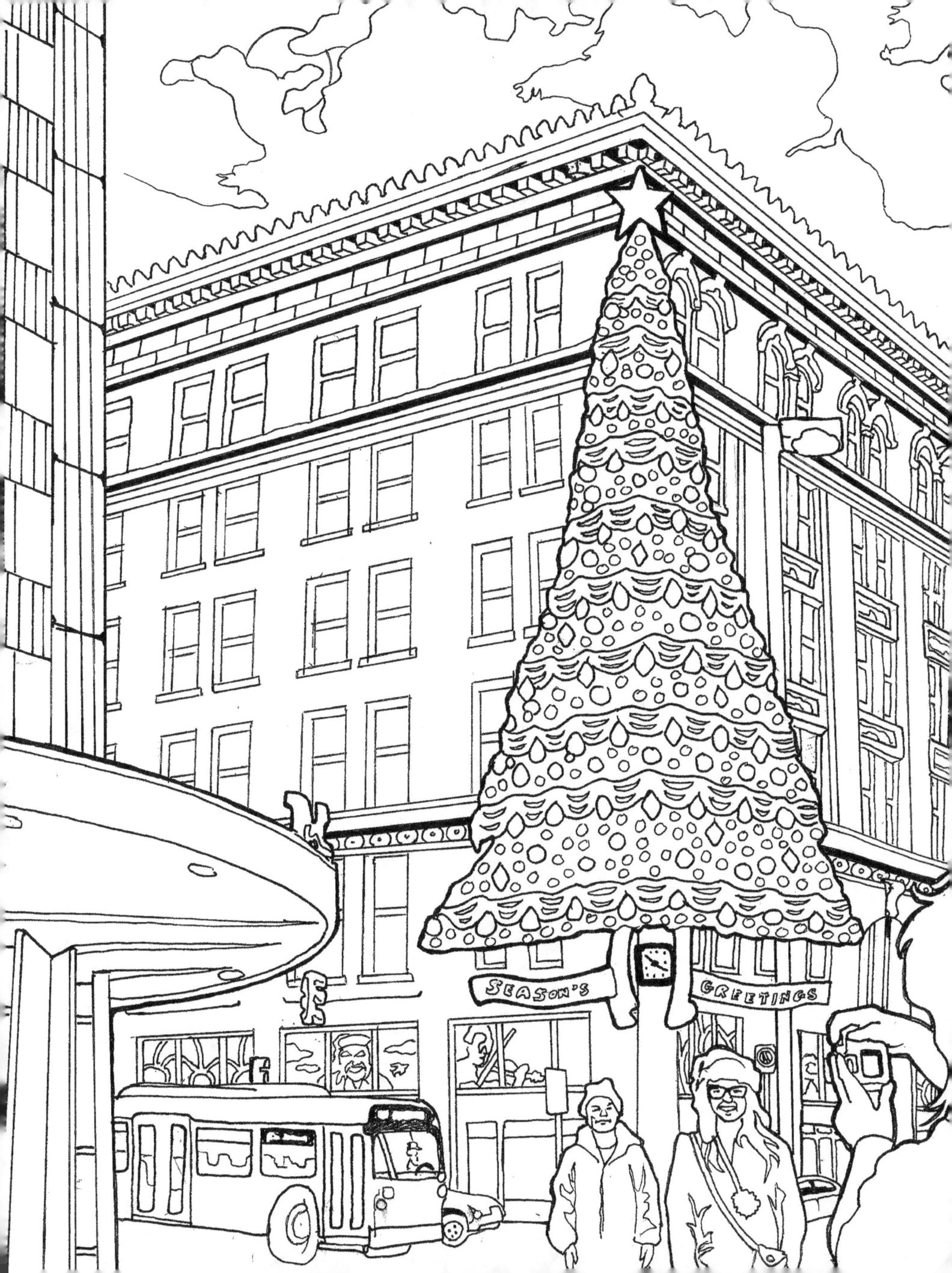

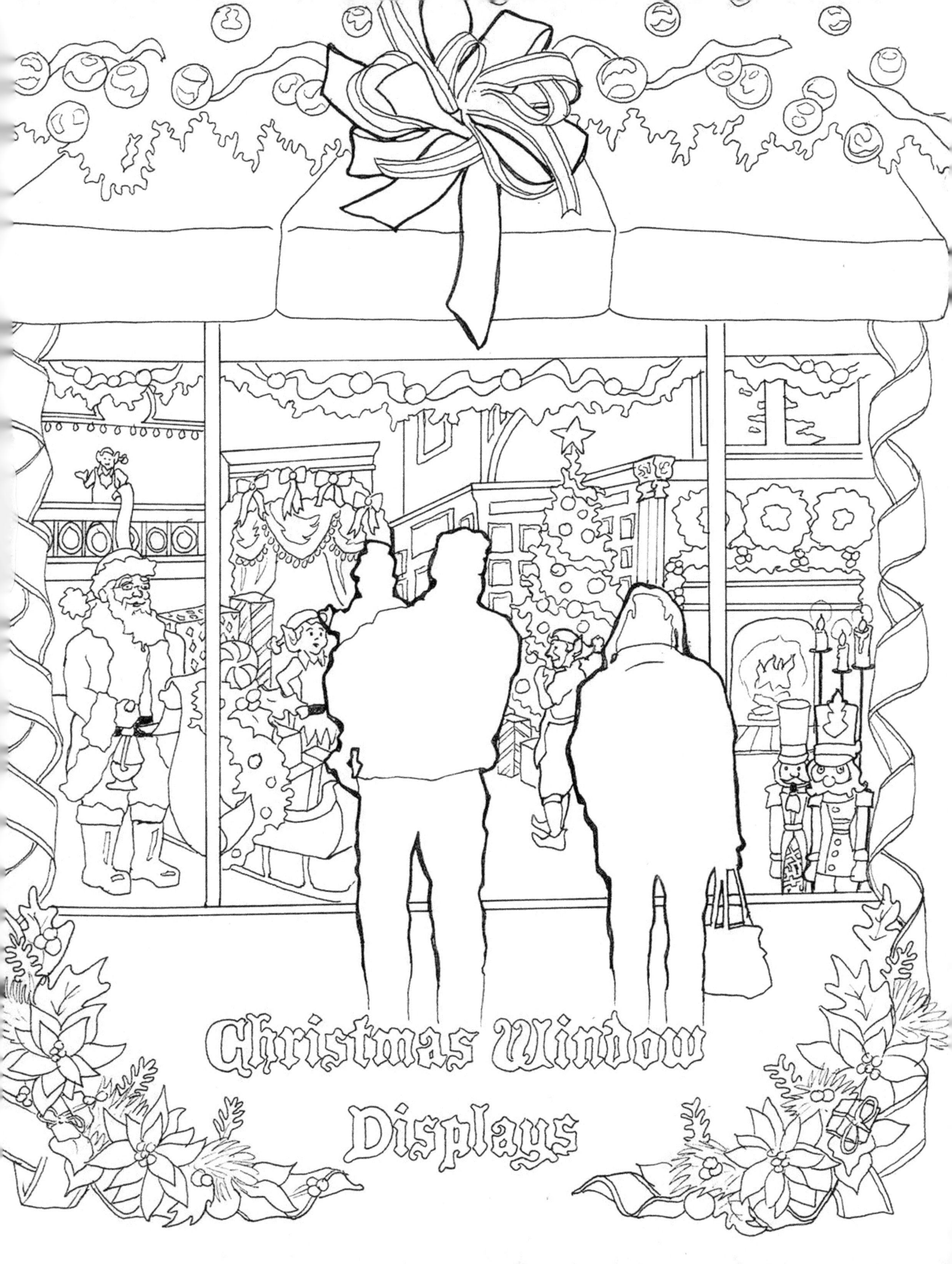

Christmas Window
Displays

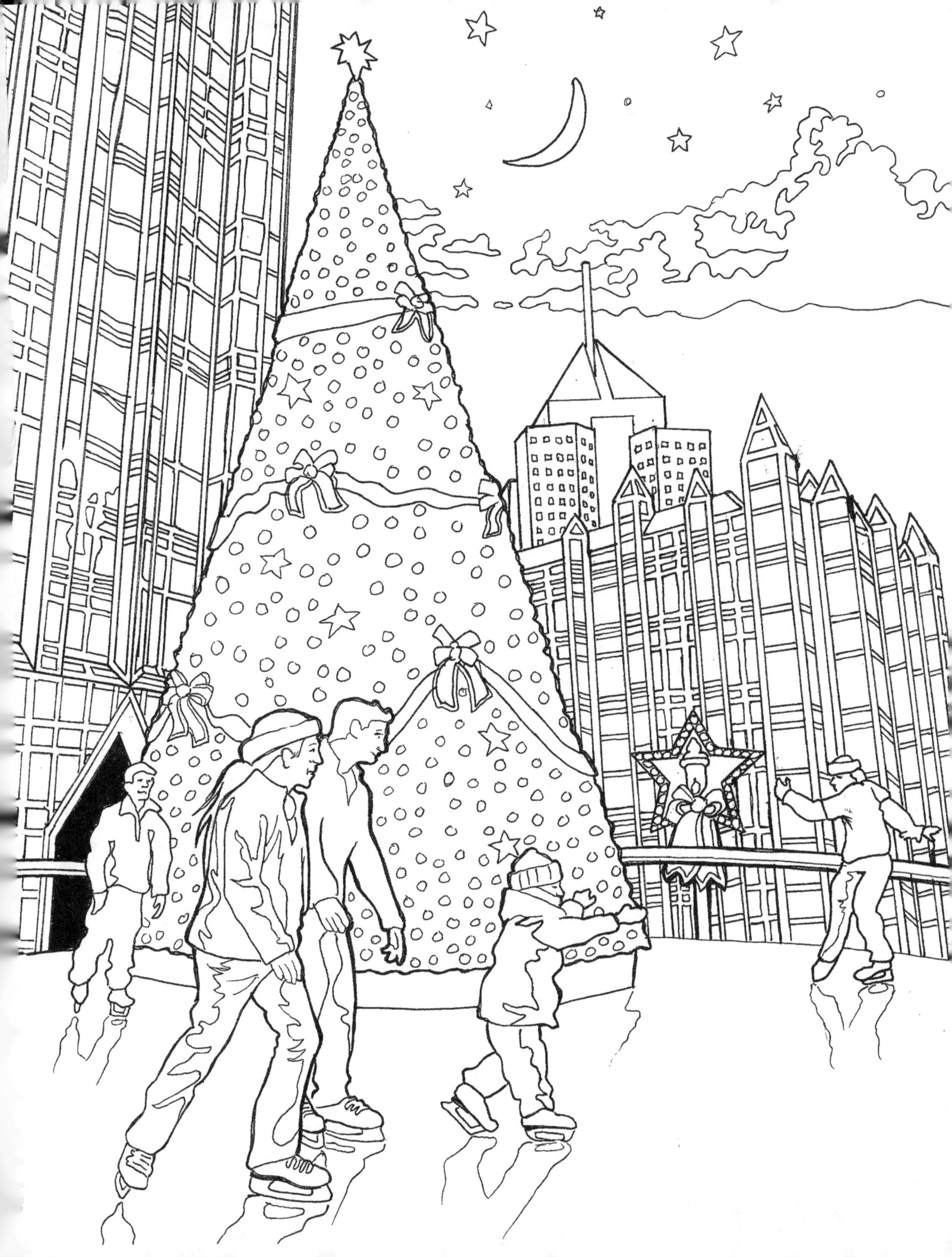